I0087044

Mama Said...

Sage Advice from "Mama" About How to Avoid Unhealthy Relationships

By

'Joyous' Janice G. Pettigrew

Copyright © 2016

All rights reserved. No part of this publication may be reproduced, stored in a retrieval system, or transmitted in copying, recording, or otherwise, without the prior written permission of the copyright owner.

ISBN: 978-0-692-37680-5

Mama Said...

Nuggets of Wisdom

Introduction

Thank you so much for picking up this little book of wisdom. Many of our Mamas have tried to impart to us nuggets of wisdom over the years. I've decided to share a few of the nuggets of wisdom passed to me and my sister from our Mama. It's not a big book and it won't take you hours to read but what you'll find inside might just save you from a world of hurt when it comes to achieving and maintaining a healthy relationship.

Think about it. From the moment you realized you'd developed an interest in boys you've had to battle to be in a relationship that is supportive, respectful, loving and most important of all safe.

Let's delve into this all the way by my first asking you a couple of questions....

First, are you finding yourself repeating a familiar yet uncomfortable cycle in your relationships?

Secondly, when it's just you and your heart is broken again, do you quietly say to yourself... Mama Said"?

Come on be honest. I will if you will. Over the years as I've gone through relationships my Mama's words have come back to haunt me. Had I taken her nuggets of wisdom to heart I know without a doubt that I could have avoided a lot of disappointment and would not have had to deal with:

Low Self-Worth

Low-Self-Esteem

Physical and Emotional Abuse

Embarrassment

Frustration

I readily admit that when I reached my teen years I suddenly woke up one morning and decided my Mama didn't know what she was talking about. Besides it had been a long time since she was a teenager. The rules she lived by didn't apply to me. How wrong was I!

Mama wanted me to <u>not</u> experience some of the things she had. She wanted me to learn from her...

Now that I'm a mother and a grandmother, I find myself in her same position. I'm sure my children and grandchildren have those moments when they think to themselves, 'Mama Said' or 'Grandma Said'.

Yes, it's true that we all have to live our own lives, however, if we take the time to really listen to what our Mamas tried to teach us we could avoid so much pain.

Sometimes it seems like we're determined to learn from the "school of hard knocks"! This puts us in the position of spending time shaking off the negative thoughts and feelings of shame, regret, remorse and embarrassment all because we didn't listen to Mama.

I know, not everyone is blessed with a mama to share their nuggets of wisdom. But there are grandmas, aunties, big sisters and mentors that if you take the time to open your ears close your mouth and open your heart to those willing to share you'll be all the wiser for it.

It's not rocket science but if taken to heart the next few chapters can propel you into a new dimension of being. I hope you'll enjoy and put into practice.

Nugget #1

Know You Better than Others Do

It took me a long time to really understand what Mama meant by this. I had to experience some devastating and sometimes horrific things in order to realize the truth behind this statement.

I say this because in my teens and early adult years I found myself in situations that were not good. As a matter of fact in some instances the emotional and physical harm caused lasted for many more years. Since I didn't know myself I became a *follower* as well as being someone needing to *please* others. All of this was done in an attempt to **"have friends"**.

By not valuing myself I short changed me and ultimately gave others permission to do the same. I didn't look in the mirror and see the beautiful me looking back. I quickly surmised that others' opinions of me had to be right and I just needed to fix the problem(s) so I could be accepted. I remember many days looking at me and calling me four-eyes, ugly, skinny and dumb.

Use my example of what not to do. Don't get caught up in trying to fit in. Spend time, quality time with yourself. It's never too late to make a change for the better. If you don't know yourself or establish your own belief system, then someone else will pull your strings and you'll end up being a puppet instead of the person you really are. Sure you'll make mistakes but they will be your mistakes and not based on someone else's opinions.

For me one of my first mistakes resulted in my trusting when I should have been cautious, all because I wanted a friend. This led to my disobeying my parents' rule and instead of going straight home after school I was some place I shouldn't have been. This led to being gang-raped at 13. The effects caused me to shrink into myself and not trust either males or females.

Another negative effect was my going through a period of promiscuity that only led to several bad choices and decisions. I can honestly admit this now for so many years I was in denial of how this incident affected me.

Make no mistake about it. Your decisions and choices carry a lot of weight and can steep you deep into depression if not tackled. You deserve better so do better and demand better of yourself and others.

Even in adulthood there were instances in which I heard myself think, 'Mama Said'…. "Know *You* Better than Others Do and Know Your Worth". I devalued myself for a very long time. Not anymore of course, because I have learned from the error of my ways, but I do have the scars to show for the hard learned lesson.

There were times I wished that I could I have turned back the clock and listened to Mama. It would have prevented me from experiencing some really tough situations. But then in another way I don't wish that. I know that's very contradictory but I wouldn't be able to help someone else were it not for the experiences of my past. The scars are there but they don't hurt and no longer have power over me. I use them instead to be a beacon of hope for others.

The saving grace is that Mama knew I'd finally learned this lesson before she passed in 2006. I do my best to pass these lessons on to my granddaughters. Will they listen? I can't say, but I have to try.

How about you? Do you know you better than others do and know your self-worth? Not sure. Then perhaps you need to examine these statements:

✓ I am not comfortable standing up for what I believe is right.

✓ I spend most of my time with people who define my self-worth.

✓ I depend on others to satisfy my needs.

If these three statements ring true to you then all I can say is flash back and see if there's a 'Mama Said' moment that can put you back on the right track. If not, please let my Mama's words sink into your being and become a part of the new you.

Start walking with purpose and knowledge that you are worthy and deserve the best. In other words spend quality time with you so that no one can ever make the mistake of dictating to you who you are or should be.

Nugget #2

Carry Yourself with Dignity & Respect

The first time I heard this from my Mama was when I was nine years old and had run all the way home from the school playground because I was bleeding. It was at that time Mama taught me about the transition from being a child to becoming a young woman. I admit I didn't fully understand the things she was telling me. It all sounded so strange.

This transition into womanhood herald a new me. I could no longer run outside in carefree abandon like my sister and brothers. It was as if overnight I became my Mama's mini-me. Suddenly I had to cast off childish things and take on a new role and responsibilities. Mama expected me to keep my siblings out of trouble and make them mind while she and Daddy worked to take care of us.

Yes, I was resentful. My childhood was gone and I didn't like it.

Now don't get me wrong. Mama didn't tell me I had to totally stop all those things it just seemed that I somehow made the decision this was expected of me. Now I began to spend more time inside, cooking, cleaning and making everybody do homework and take baths. It was with these new responsibilities that a small voice inside said 'being an adult is no fun'.

No wonder my parents argued a lot and hardly smiled. That's what I said. I was not equipped to understand the complexities of being an adult let alone a parent. Either way the thought never left me.

By the time I started high school I'd been going through my monthly cycle for almost four years. I knew what to expect. There was the pain, bloating, the need to be cautious so as to not ruin my clothes and to make sure that my most private area always smelled and felt clean and fresh.

I thought I was doing a good job carrying myself with dignity and respect. Boy was I way off base. For years I blamed my promiscuity on what happened to me at 13 but honestly that's not entirely true. I know now there were opportunities to change my behavior, I made the decision to not change. That decision cost me dearly.

Think about this: Respecting myself would have prevented me from allowing boys to persuade me to think so little of the precious jewel I had. Sure it was taken violently once but all the other times that followed with the exception of another incident in my early twenties I chose to give away.

Not only did I give my "jewels" away, but I silently gave permission to be disrespected in other ways. For instance, whenever I answered to a name my parents didn't give me I opened the door to disrespect a little wider.

How about you? Can you think of instances when you did the same?

Sure in our young minds we persuaded ourselves to believe that it was cute and it made us feel special. I'm sure our grownup selves now know the cruel truth.

Mama used to say, "A young lady would never expose her body in ways that drew unwanted attention from the opposite sex". I didn't believe her. Halter tops and short shorts were the things to wear. Anything else made me a square! When I look at what some young girls walk out of the house wearing (or not wearing!) I shake my head and I'm reminded of what… 'Mama Said'.

Even the amount of makeup tells a story and sometimes the story may not be nice. Personally I didn't have that to worry about. I was never good at putting on makeup. Even today I may put on a little lipstick and call it a day. On very special occasions I will wear more than that. I can vividly recall how the girls in school started to experiment with makeup. Some looked nice others however looked well let's just say, 'Mama Said', "less is more".

There were so many things I took for granted which resulted in my not respecting me the way I deserved. Let's see if any of these sound familiar to you. 'Mama Said':

- ✓ If you're worth taking out…let the boy (man) come to the door;

- ✓ A gentleman always opens the door and allows you to walk through first;

- ✓ If you're riding in a car he should open the door for you (getting in or out);

- ✓ Let him pull out your chair and seat you first;

- ✓ Caught in a rainstorm without an umbrella he should offer you his coat;

- ✓ A kiss on the cheek is sufficient for a first date;

- ✓ Never be the only girl in the group;

I never thought much about having a date pull up and honk their horn. That was my signal to hurry up let's get going. Foolishly I thought it meant they were so excited to see me that I needed to come on! As I've matured I appreciate the respect of having the man come to the door, ring the door bell and wait patiently for me to answer.

It actually gives me goose bumps. Okay, sure I'm an 'ole' married woman now but to have my husband think enough of me to escort me out the door is such a cherished pleasure!

With young people I rarely see males opening the door and allow the female to walk through first. It seems to be a 'me' first attitude. Okay I must admit even older adults don't do it often. I always smile when I see it being done and it makes me hold my head higher with a soft smile on my face when my husband does it.

I've even had to wait patiently while he allowed other women to walk through. Of course I raise an eye-brow when I see her walk through and her male companion does too. Somehow I always felt he should have allowed my husband through and then himself. I'm just saying.

The point Mama was making about the door was that the man should show that common courtesy. It's a big sign of RESPECT.

Now it was a long time before I was riding in a car to experience having the man hold the door open for me let alone come around when he's parked to open my door for me to get out. Here's a hint though, if he happens to have a car that doesn't have automatic locks then Mama used to say the woman should reach across and unlock his door. Strange I remember seeing that in a movie once. Can't recall the name but I remember it made me smile.

The first time I went to a restaurant on a date I stood waiting for my escort to pull out my chair. It didn't happen so I just sat down. When the waitress arrived to take our order he quickly ordered his food and then asked what I'd like. In my head I could clearly hear Mama and I don't think she was pleased. Actually neither was I. But I was young and figured those things didn't matter anymore. WRONG!

Even now when my husband and I go out to eat whether it's a fancy place or the neighborhood fast food place he always waits for me to order my food. If we are eating there he wipes the table even if it's been cleaned already. Okay, yes it's the little things that make me smile.

Mama did say he was the best 'almost son-n-law' she ever had long before we tied the knot. That was Mama's way of giving her stamp of approval. Mama didn't say much but she observed a lot. Even during my rebellious age so I know she had to have been doing a lot of praying for this wayward daughter of hers. I'm grateful and I'm sure she's looking down from heaven and still giving me a thumbs-up sign.

Caught in a rainstorm! This one I thought would never happen to me. After all I always carried an umbrella in my bag, purse or car and was usually the one sharing it. One day it did happen and I was pleasantly surprised to have the gentleman offer his raincoat. That was many, many, moons ago but it definitely reminded me of one of my 'Mama Said'… sayings.

A kiss on the cheek is sufficient for a first date was very foreign to me. Especially for several years after being violated the way I was. It wasn't until I began to think differently about myself that this nugget of wisdom from Mama made sense to me. Before then I didn't value myself the way I should and opened the door for a lot of misunderstanding, mistrust and mistreatment. After all Mama did say, "If you give it all away what special gift do you have to offer to the right person?" Gives you food for thought doesn't it?

I made a lot of mistakes back then. I try to school my granddaughters and the young ladies I work with through the Precious Jewel Program so they don't have to experience that. Of course with all the young girls who are too young to be having babies having babies there's still a lot of work to be done. And not just with young girls, older women need a reminder of what 'Mama Said'.

I've heard all kinds of reasons (excuses) for doing the opposite but if we're really honest we must admit we've allowed social media, movies, celebrities and the like to skew our perceptions of ourselves. We don't have to follow the accepted behavior we can set standards that are appropriate for us. We've lost ourselves! Let's get it back! And teach our daughters, granddaughters, and all young women better.

Never be the only girl in the group – I know there are a lot of tomboys out there but really shouldn't we still reinforce this? I know I do and so does my husband. I'll never forget many years ago when his daughter came to visit she happened to meet a young man she'd known when she was younger; he invited her to his house and of course she asked her dad to take her. Yes she was grown, graduated from high school and had a child. But that didn't stop him intervening when he deemed it appropriate.

When they arrived at the location he sat and observed the surroundings. Suddenly his antenna went into overdrive. Before his daughter could make another step towards the building he leaned over and told her to get back in the car.

As you can imagine she was not happy but as he explained to her what he saw was not good. He didn't see another female only about five or six guys.

I remember him bringing her back to the house and hearing her protesting loudly that she could take care of herself. His comeback was "Not on my watch". She huffed and puffed and gave him the silent treatment for a good 2 years. It was a few years later before she finally admitted he did the right thing.

There's nothing wrong with having male friends. No one is saying differently. What I am saying is that it's up to us to protect ourselves and it starts by not being in a situation that could become compromising and/or dangerous.

Whether you're an adult or a young teen you don't want to be placed in a predicament that could lead to unanticipated consequences. Like 'Mama Said', "You should never be the only girl in the group".

Nugget #3

You Can't Change another Human Being

I was 22 years old when Mama first shared this nugget of truth. We were sitting on the front porch watching my two little boys playing in the yard. I'd finally gotten up the courage to tell her what I was experiencing at home. I shared my frustration and my belief that all I had to do to make it better was to do better.

I was old enough then for Mama to share a little more about her and Daddy's relationship. I remembered that there were fights between them when I was growing up and somewhere in the back of my mind I blamed Mama. I assumed that maybe if she stayed home and cooked and cleaned there wouldn't be any fights.

Now I was of course doing exactly that and yet still experiencing the same thing. Obviously that was not the secret to a happy marriage. I learned that Mama stayed because it's what her generation did. But she did not want that for me or any of her children. Eventually she broke from that tradition and my parents went their separate ways.

'Mama Said' real love:

- ✓ Does not cause pain physically or emotionally

- ✓ Warms you through and through

- ✓ Protects you

- ✓ Cherishes you

- ✓ Caresses not hit

- ✓ Kisses not slap

- ✓ Lights up your face with joy

- ✓ Makes you giggle

- ✓ Thinks of the other person first

- ✓ Honors in words and deed

Mama was a very wise woman. I can admit it now without my haughty attitude of a teenager. Although my stubbornness caused me to learn these lessons later rather than sooner I hope you'll be a little wiser than me. It took me three tries to get it right and it's going on 30 years of real love (I'm talking about my marriage).

Again I'm grateful Mama knew I'd learned the lesson before she passed. It still brings a smile to my face to remember her calling Oscar 'the best almost son-n-law' she ever had. She beamed with pride the day we walked down the aisle as husband and wife.

Let's look at Mama's list a little closer:

Does not cause pain physically or emotionally – It took two failed marriages for me to get this. I hope you'll get it now. You're not a child. You don't need to be raised again. If someone has to berate you to feel better about him or herself then they don't belong in your orbit. I'm from the old school and corporal punishment was a way of life with my parents. That being said there was absolutely no reason for a man to put a hand on me. I didn't need re-raising.

In my first marriage I experienced a lot of physical and emotional abuse. Shame caused me to keep it a secret. Self-doubt and feelings of worthlessness also played a part. Each stripped me of my self-confidence and plunged me into a dark world where I didn't belong. I didn't see the light I didn't see me only the shell of me and it wasn't pretty.

For so long I'd made excuses for the swollen bleeding lips, the bruises on my arms and even once a black eye. During those times I had no thought of believing that this isn't right. I was in survivor's mode and it took all I had. There were of course glimpses of the person my husband used to be but eventually the time between him and the other person began to grow shorter and shorter. The butterflies in the pit my stomach seemed to always be just at the surface and I couldn't control them. Before I knew it I was constantly at the ready trying to figure out what to do in order to avoid any physical or emotional pain.

One day I suffered emotional and physical abuse in front of my boys. They were six and seven at the time. The look of fear and panic in their eyes woke the fighter in me. I knew I never wanted then to see their father abuse me in that way ever again. When he stormed out of the house I grabbed my boys and gently cooed to them that everything would be alright.

That's the day I went to my parents' house and finally shared with Mama what I'd been going through. She didn't take an 'I told you so attitude', but I remember thinking, 'Mama said, love does not cause pain physically or emotionally'.

Mama had my two oldest brothers go back to my apartment and help me pack some things to bring back to her house. I would stay back in my old room with the boys until I was able to get my own apartment. I was able to accomplish that in about three weeks. Lesson learned, right. WRONG.

Had it been so easy I'm certain marriage number two would have never happened. I was needy he was needy and about 10 years older. I traveled that road once more of physical and emotional abuse coupled with isolation and financial blackmail. Wow, I was a hard knot and I've the scars to prove it. I use them now to teach my granddaughters and others.

Warms you through and through – Has just being in the same room with someone caused you to feel as if you'd just drank a hot cup of cocoa and the warmth seems to travel throughout your body? No. Don't you want to?

30 plus years later and there are times in the middle of the day I'll think of Oscar and the warmth travels from my face to the pit of stomach and below. My heart quickens with excitement and puts a goofy smile on my face. I'm pretty sure some of my coworkers may have wondered from time to time, 'What's up with Janice.' If they only knew!

There are times just for the heck of it I'll sit next to him on the sofa and lay my head on his shoulder. It feels so good. There are other times when I have my head on his chest and can feel his heartbeat. I swear it feels as if our hearts are beating in tune to each other.

It feels so wonderful to be with someone who truly loves you and you have absolutely no fear that he would ever hurt you physically or emotionally. After 30 plus years I can count the number of heated arguments on one hand with fingers left over. That is such a welcomed change from the chaos of the past.

Protects you – Another human being without even giving it great thought will want to protect you if they truly love you. Never would they want to be the catalyst to cause you harm. It's not easy to let go of the reins after an unhealthy relationship and let another human being look out for you. If you ever meet my husband I'm sure he'll have some stories to tell of breaking down my walls. But break them he did.

I have no doubt that Oscar will protect me. He's been doing it for years now. Sometimes he's even had to protect me from myself. But that's another story.

Traveling through this life we've been to places that from the outside seemed a bit wary. Yet because of the person I'm with I have no fear. The self-confidence my husband exudes gives me confidence. The feel of his protective hand at the small of my back lets me know without words that I'm safe and secure. The firm grip as we hold hands tells me 'I got you' and so I am free to be. After all Mama Said…

Cherishes you – To cherish is to love, protect, and care for someone or something that is important to you. Shouldn't you be cherished by the one you love? It should be natural not forced.

In many of my past relationships I lacked the feeling of being cherished. It was foreign to me. As a matter of fact I didn't even know it was missing. I didn't do a lot of dating in my day. I married very early had kids, divorced and then remarried all before I was even 30 years old.

This concept of being cherished had no meaning to me but on that front porch talking to Mama, I remember 'Mama Said…' and so I began to believe. I learned you can't make another human being cherish you. But you can cherish yourself.

If you cherish yourself then you'll be careful of the people you allow within your circle. You will not stand to be mistreated, abused and degraded. Cherishing yourself will not allow you to suffer indignity.

When you cherish you it's as if you are your own child and will do all you can to make sure this child (you) always knows just how special and precious you are. There's a quiet confident way you walk that signals to others you are not to be trifled with. Your heart is open for real relationships but closed to anything less.

Caresses not hit – The touch of your loved one should be sweet, gentle and filled with love. Anything less is not love and should be discarded. Oh if only I'd paid closer attention when Mama was doling out her nuggets of wisdom. Perhaps the time spent in the valley of despair could have been shortened.

Too many times to count do I recall the sting of a raised hand on my check and the tears and pain that followed. How could I have ever for a moment believed this behavior was LOVE??? Perhaps the greatest answer is that I for one had no concept of what LOVE really was. Mama tried to tell me. I chose to ignore her and suffered the consequences.

Anyone man or woman should not see bruises or scars received at the hands of someone who proclaims to love them. I can't stand to pinch myself, why would I want to have any part of me touched so violently! The gentle caress of my husband's hands makes me tingle. I wouldn't trade that for anything.

Kisses not slap – See Above: A slap is pain no matter how you look at it. Don't mistake it for anything else. 'It was just a little thing', right and the next time will it be a fist?

Done hard enough a slap could loosen teeth, injure an eye and definitely leave a mark long after the slap. It will last so long that you just may see the imprint of the hand that did it on your face days later. Been there done that in my past life.

I love kisses! I love when Oscar plants them on my nose, forehead, ear, neck, shoulder and of course on my lips. Just thinking about it makes me smile. Think I'll go and get me some now.

Lights up your face with joy – After all these years in my quiet moments I think of my husband and it makes me smile. Sure we have days as I lovingly tell him I don't like him but loving him is forever and it gives me great joy. There are times when I see him sneak a look my way and it makes me smile for though I may have a little more of me to love, LOVE is all I see when I look into his eyes.

Makes you giggle – Together we have 30 grandkids and 4 great-grandkids even so there's still a kid in us as well. There are times my giggles (laughter) can be heard outside from behind closed doors. Oscar does that to me. The grandkids tease us and say we need help. We say, why? Feels fine to us!

I admit I do have a hearty laugh and it can't be faked. Oscar can bring that out of me and it feels wonderful. Of course that's not the only way he makes me giggle.

Don't worry sweetie, I won't give all your secrets away. But I do have to share this.

There are days I come home from work and I'm tired. Yes, I sit behind a desk all day but I have very sensitive feet. They can make me moan in pain. Oscar will gently take each and massage them. In between fits of giggles I relax so much so that give me 15 minutes and I'm out for the count. A giggle, a foot-massage and a kiss on the forehead is all it takes. What a way to end the day!

Thinks of the other person first – A long time before meeting the Mr. Right that God had for me I spent so much time thinking of myself and the kids that when Mr. Right (Oscar) came along I still had a few lessons to learn. I learned them too, simply by watching his actions. Now it's natural and feels really good. You see when you think of the other person first then you want the best for them. Interestingly enough if you want the best for them then the best for you soon follows. It becomes automatic you don't have to force it.

Honors in words and deed – Enough said. The actions of the other person give credibility to these words. I know without a doubt that the words my husband says are true and honorable.

We as women tend to think it's our job to fix others especially in our relationships. But as Mama was so fond of telling me, "A man has already been raised you either accept him or move on". Sometimes I know this can be hard to do. In the end this advice is a treasure. The majority of men already have their minds made up on any number of subjects including how they treat members of the opposite sex and whether or not they're marriage material. No matter how hard you try you cannot influence him to be anyone other than who he is. Of course you can complement those positive traits he already has.

Before investing in a relationship that may not be going anywhere have you really listened to the words that come out of his mouth? Those words are revealing and though he may pretend for a while that's hard work. Eventually the truth will surface; maybe not in words but definitely in deed. Your deeds reveal the depth of your being and can't be denied. What about your deeds are they in character with the person you want to be?

I've heard women say, 'he just needs a little understanding', or 'I know he loves me he just doesn't know how to show it'. Really!

May I suggest working on you and your faults, flaws, short-comings and positive attributes? If you're busy doing that then you don't have time to try and change another human being. If you have been blessed to have children or interact with children on a regular basis then use that time to affect positive change in them.

Like Mama Said... You can't change another human being.

Nugget # 4

"No" is Not a Bad Word

I can't tell you the number of times I heard Mama say this. Yet so many times I found myself saying '*Yes*' when what I really meant and wanted to say was **'No'**.

There's the time a boy asked to walk me home, but asked if we could stop at his house first?

Or the time a man offered me a ride home.

The time a guy asked for my phone number.

The time someone said to me, 'Try it you'll like'.

Hey can I talk to you, after whistling at me when I walked by.

Can I stay with you for a while?

If I had made the decision at any one of those times I could have saved myself from heartache, tragic circumstances, guilt, or even worse, fear of rejection. We as women allow ourselves to be placed in situations

27

we are not prepared to handle. A simple 'no' can be a life saver.

It's okay to say no I will not answer to something other than my name. This will help to ensure that you do not allow others to belittle you with words that are condescending, crass, vulgar or just plain wrong. My name is Janice I will answer to 'Joyous' Janice, Mama, Grandma or sweetheart from my husband. Anything else and well I don't know you.

The word 'No' to a ride from a stranger could save you from being raped and battered in a secluded area (I speak from experience). Say 'No' to allowing a man to stay with you for a 'few days'. It may well save you from losing control of your own living space.

Say 'No', to giving your phone number to every person who asks. It just could save you from a stalker or worse.

These are just a few examples from my own life. Mama's words of wisdom ring true even today. So, how about you? Do you have real life examples of when, 'No' was the appropriate response?

In many ways we are conditioned to say yes, to bend to the will and wishes of others. Here's something to think about however. When the word yes gets ready to flow from your lips are you at peace? Or do you suddenly have sweaty palms, rapid heartbeat or fear? It you do then it's highly likely that the correct response should be a resounding NO.

The word 'No' doesn't make you mean, selfish or uncaring. It is simply your guide to ensure that you are whole. 'No' at the appropriate time opens the door for a real 'yes'. So use that word with authority.

After all Mama Said…'No' is not a bad word!

Nugget #5

Change Your Thinking Change Your Outcome

Our minds can play tricks on us. It can cause us to doubt our own sanity. It can even cause us to doubt our worth. I admit that for many years I didn't believe in myself. I based my self-worth and abilities on the thinking of others. It was only after I began to reject others' opinions as the WHOLE TRUTH about me was I able to rewire my thinking.

Before then I allowed previous relationships to dictate what I would and/or would not accept. The vast majority of the time it left me feeling worthless or a non-person.

When I began to believe in myself and that I deserved so much more than what I had been receiving I found myself rejecting the type of men that used to gravitate to me. No longer would I accept that another human being knew best when it came to what I wore, ate thought or believed.

It was by changing my thinking that I began to rediscover the person that had been hidden screaming to be let out.

I began to love my quirks. From my kooky laugh to reading books that allowed my imagination to flow.

My changed thinking told me I was worthy and that I was valuable to ME. And by valuing myself I no longer went with the flow. It was okay to be alone. Besides if I enjoyed my own company how could I even think that I was lonely or alone?

Changing my thinking put me in a position to recognize and accept positive influences in my life. I was able to let go of toxic relationships. Sometimes this even meant loving family from afar.

I found myself, laughing more, being a better mom, friend, sister and employee. I began to reignite desires for my life that had nearly been snuffed out from misuse, mistreatment and denial. My passion for writing grew and of course my desire to help others overcome adversity in their lives in order to be the person they were always meant to be.

By changing my thinking I could look in the mirror and say, 'hello beautiful'. I could look in my eyes and really see me looking back. There was light there and maybe a twinkle of mischief.

My new way of thinking gave me permission to dream past my present circumstances and make a move to bring those dreams to reality. My new way of thinking had a positive influence on my boys as well. They saw a Mama who was brave, smart, and funny, still stern but Mama walked with confidence. They recognized that the old Mama was gone and this new improved version had time for them and spent quality time just listening and teaching.

My changed thinking allowed me to soar further than what society had dictated. I looked forward to the future instead of dreading it. It was the greatest thing I could have done.

The status quo was no longer allowed to reside in my being or in my presence. After all Mama Said… change your thinking, change your outcome.

Nugget #6

Prepare for Him Before He Arrives

This sounds so simple yet it isn't. It requires action on your part. You can't expect Mr. Right to miraculously appear if you have not done all you can to be the best Ms. Right.

So how can you accomplish this? May I suggest you begin by taking inventory of yourself? You need to honestly evaluate the person currently residing in your body. Begin by making 3 lists:

Positive   Negative   Things to Improve

By being honest you can begin to transform into the best 'you' that you can be. You must decide if the positives truly are positives and whether the negatives hinder or harm you. As for the list of 'Things to Improve' I dare you to say there's nothing to improve. If you're a living, breathing individual them there's always something to improve upon.

For me I had a very long list of things in each column. Let me share a few:

Under positive I had, hard worker, friend, giver and caring just to name a few. Under negative I was easily led by others, timid, hate confrontation and cried easily.

Under things to improve I had, learn to speak up, stand up for what's right, be self-confident.

All three lists were much longer I'm simply sharing a few just to give you an idea. You see those positive attributes served me well when Mr. Right finally came along. Relationships can be messy. Things are not always rosy so you need to be well equipped to handle whatever life throws your way.

The negative attributes gave way to the things I needed to improve upon. For example being self-confident gave rise to a woman who would stand beside Mr. Right through the rough patch and be there to support and defend if needed.

I thought long and hard about the ideal mate. There were some typical attributes all women seek but that is only surface stuff. Besides after two failed marriages and a host of other unhealthy relationships perhaps it was time to take a step back and look at ME.

I had to ask myself, what type of woman am I really? Am I ready for a serious relationship? If not what do I need to do? Sure there were loads of books on the subject but when you think about it that's still based on someone else's opinion. It was about time for me to dig deep and uncover ME for ME. By doing that I was certain to be ready when Mr. Right came along.

I needed to be in position to receive the good so it was time to empty out the baggage that had been holding me back. Wow, that was a lot of work. I had to deal with forgiveness, honesty, hard work, cleanliness, patience, dependability and faith. Making over the old Janice was exhausting at times but very rewarding.

Don't get me wrong it wasn't all completed by the time Mr. Right appeared but I was well on my way. Just ask Oscar. A healthy relationship is not a 2-way street. Be sure you're traveling in the same direction.

The only way to be absolutely sure is to work on you. Only you know you and what's needed you don't need to beat yourself up just be honest. When the work is done you will be pleased.

Remember Mama Said…prepare for him before he arrives.

Nugget #7

Be Specific

We all developed an idea of what our Mr. Right would be like. However we tend to merely scratch the surface and actually leave ourselves open for disappointment and failure.

We should be as specific as possible. Sure you have some ideas about the type of man you're looking for but have you really thought about everything? After all, looks will change with the passage of time and of course superficial traits will disappoint you every time.

Ask yourself when the hard times come will your ideal man be there? Will he be there when you're sick or when you lose your income?

Is he or will he be a positive influence in your children's lives? Will he think of you and love you as much as he loves himself and God? Does he value your opinions, your individuality or does he spend ALL his time remaking you into his ideal mate? Go back to chapter 3 and look at that list again of things that 'Mama said'.

✓ Does not cause pain physically or emotionally

✓ Warms you through and through

✓ Protects you

✓ Cherishes you

✓ Caresses not hit

✓ Kisses not slap

✓ Lights up your face with joy

✓ Makes you giggle

✓ Thinks of the other person first

✓ Honors in words and deed

Can you check these requirements off as you're seeking Mr. Right? Better yet stop seeking. Prepare yourself and Mr. Right will surely find you and you'll know it without a shadow of doubt when he has arrived.

Make sure you're looking for long term not just a thrill for the moment. Be certain you are putting your best self out there. After all you both could be the most beautiful people in to world on the outside. The key is to ensure that the inside also reflects that beauty.

Thus it's important to be specific when it comes to describing the man of your dreams. Not just a dream but your desire and need. Hint: Need in this case does not mean usury.

What's the use of having a man who knows how to make money if he doesn't know how to love, honor, cherish and respect you?

Does the man that knows how to use words that make your stomach quiver and curl your toes also know how to be in a relationship when the hard times come? Those words are no comfort when you're battling an illness and need your man to be there to hold your hand, wipe your brow or get your medicine. He can't help you if he's at the pool hall or bar with his friends.

There's an old saying of if you want to know how a man will treat you observe how he treats his Mama. Some say it's not true. In my case when I observed this fine man who's in my life now that saying is definitely true.

I saw first-hand the love and respect Oscar had for his Mama. I saw how gently he treated her and how he spoke softly. I watched him take lotion and massage his Mama's feet because she said they hurt. I smiled at the look of pleasure on her face as he did it. Foot massage, hey I get those!

Another important trait for me was to have a man who believed in God and was not ashamed to show it. I got that in spades. It has only strengthened my own faith.

No one can tell you what your specific requirements should be. That's up to you just make sure you're not just scratching the surface. Think long term not immediate with an eye towards a bright future. No half-stepping. It'll cost you!

Years after my second failed marriage but before Oscar came along Mama Said...I needed to be specific about the type of man I desired to be in my life. Check, check and check!

Nugget #8

Love Yourself

If you don't love yourself how can you expect to love another? When you love yourself you have given permission for the universe to reward you with unmistakable joy.

After all when you love yourself you won't be a second class individual. Only the best will do. This is not being conceited but reinforcing your new thinking that you will not allow yourself to be abused, degraded or physically harmed.

Loving yourself says I am worthy. It brings you to a state of peace and tranquility. You'll be open to positives and the right people in your life.

I remember before truly loving myself I thought it was awesome to get cat calls when I walk down the street. Loving myself has released me to acknowledge just how wrong that kind of thinking was.

Loving me says I care just as much about my inner strength and beauty as how I look on the outside. Loving me gives me permission to say 'No' with authority to anyone asking for more than what I'm willing to give. It has freed me to accept all of me faults and flaws. Loving me brings me joy. I don't have to wait for superficial approval to accept me.

Loving me raises the stakes and puts me in control. Loving me opened my eyes to my surroundings so that I could make sound, wise choices and decisions.

Loving me allowed me to be happy in my own skin and not pattern after someone else.

Loving me set the stage for Mr. Right to show up and I recognized him even though I had to play hard to get for just a little bit.

Loving me opened the door to my heart and allowed me to give the key to Mr. Right knowing without a doubt he would forever cherish and protect it.

So how do you begin to love yourself? Start by spending quality time with you. My favorite way to do that is when I journal. This is a way for me to track my progress and document the process. I've reread things I wrote years earlier and amaze myself with how limited I was in my thinking. I document that as well as the growth I've experienced since the original writing. Sometimes I've even been embarrassed by the words I jotted down;

embarrassed but not ashamed. The shame would have been if there was no evidence of growth.

I love soaking in a hot tub of suds and letting the work day melt away. I have to be careful not to get too relaxed and make the mistake of sinking too deep. I look in the mirror when I get out of the tub and admire my breasts that fed two babies. I can appreciate the hips that carried those babies so I could work and provide for them. I look at the twinkle in my eyes and appreciate the stories lurking there near the surface.

Loving me says I appreciate the scars on my body for they are a testament to the journey I've had and I look forward to the surprises still in store for me. Even more I appreciate the heart scars for they have healed and freed me to love my husband.

Loving me gives me freedom to listen quietly to jazz and allow the music to sway my body. I don't have time to be lonely for I'm busy communing with me. This prepares me to commune with hubby when he's around.

Loving me means I accept all of me and only someone who can accept me as I am is worthy to be in my orbit. Hi honey welcome to the ride of your life!

Only you know what works for you the important thing is to begin the process. After all Mama Said...Loving yourself opens a whole new world to you one in which an unhealthy relationship is not welcomed.

Nugget #9

Education is Important

I was 16 when Mama told me this. At the time I dreamed of one day becoming a lawyer. Unfortunately I got sidetracked in more ways than one. You see at 16 still thinking all of my Mama's advice wasn't good enough, I found myself pregnant and preparing for motherhood instead of doing all the things needed to go to college.

Sure I was in the top 10% of my class in 1975 even after giving birth to a little boy just a few weeks shy of my high school graduation. While my classmates were headed off to college I was at home taking care of a baby and a husband in a marriage that was filled with abuse, fear and shame.

I think I could have been a great lawyer; however my choices prevented me from finding out. And by the time my marriage had failed I had two little ones depending on me to take care of them. My desires and aspirations took a back seat to their needs.

I did take some college classes online to prove to myself that I could do it. This was of course years later after my sons were grown with children of their own.

Don't get me wrong I don't begrudge my children for the sacrifices I had to make however I know without a doubt I could have provided so much more to them had I gone on to get a higher education.

Now days there are so many ways to improve your education. You can work and still get in some college courses. You could possibly be working at a job that helps with college financing. You won't know until you ask and try.

I remember Mama had a thirst for knowledge and was always looking for ways to improve her position at work. Many nights I recall quizzing her for a test. Seeing her made me want to do better as well even after getting pregnant and marrying early.

Mama Said... Education is important because no one can take that from you. You have to earn it and in the process learn just how remarkable you are. Education opens the door for you to be self-sufficient and not relying on someone else to take care of you.

Sure in a healthy relationship there's give and take but an unhealthy one tips the scales against you. Mama Said…get your education child. Like I said I didn't listen then but it's ingrained in me now and I pass it on to all my granddaughters.

What about you? Do you have desires, goals or aspirations you'd like to achieve that require higher learning? If the answer is yes, then don't let the opportunity slip past you.

Are you stuck and unsure where to begin the process?

I have a suggestion: Visit the Fresh Start for Women website and click on the events tab we have a 6-week "Guided" online course "*From Adversity to Passion: A Journey to Your Divine Destiny and Joy*" During this 6-week course you'll begin to discover the *new you* that is waiting to come forth.

Getting an education gives you value that can't be stripped from you by anyone. Remember, 'Mama Said' – know yourself better than others and know your worth.

Nugget # 10

Put God First and He will Order Your Steps

'Mama Said', having faith in something greater than you can help avoid so many pitfalls. So often we think we have all the answers when in reality we can be so hard-headed!

Have you ever thought about doing something but there was a nagging feeling that the choice you were thinking of was wrong?

I know I have more times than I care to count. Inevitably I've paid a high price for ignoring the still small voice speaking to me.

All of us have a belief system that knows what is best for us; the question then becomes are you an active or passive believer? To me a passive believer is one who has learned a lot, but never puts that faith into action. It's never tested.

For years I was a passive believer. I went to church because that's what we did on Sundays. I sat in Bible study and listened but forgot all about it when class was over until the next Sunday. I memorized scripture and gave lip service to what was being said. But I didn't own it. I didn't make it a part of my everyday existence. I went about my business with no thought for others.

There were two significant events in my life that changed me.

1. When Mama was first diagnosed with breast cancer in 1985 I got scared. Mama and I had had lots of conversations about a lot of different things but one thing that stood out the most was her firm belief that her faith kept her going. I witnessed her go through chemo and radiation and still go to work three days a week until she was able to return to work full time. Mama shared that although she'd always believed in God it was only after being diagnosed with cancer did she move beyond simple lip-service. Cancer taught her to appreciate life more and to live it on purpose not just for herself but as an example to her family.

2. After two failed marriages and several unhealthy relationships I stopped trying. Instead, I got to know Janice again and in the process learned to love and appreciate her faults, flaws and all. When I stopped trying to make myself over to be accepted based on someone else's opinion,

then God in his infinite wisdom and a bit of humor sent the right person into my life. 30 years later we're still together.

The relationship we have is one so much like what **'Mama Said'** about real love:

✓ Does not cause pain physically or emotionally;

✓ Warms you through and through;

✓ Protects you;

✓ Cherishes you;

✓ Caresses and does not hit;

✓ Kisses and not slap;

✓ Lights up your face with joy;

✓ Makes you giggle;

✓ Thinks of the other person first;

✓ Honors in words and deed;

I don't think our relationship would be as strong were it not for the faith that has been nurtured over the years. Faith has kept me when all else seemed lost. Faith held me together when God called Mama home to be with Him and although I was angry at Him for a while he didn't hold it against me. Faith was my rock when I was unemployed more than two and a half years.

When I've felt lost or needed a listening ear not only do I have my husband but because of my Faith I am able to draw strength, comfort and guidance from God.

My Faith is not passive, I have a very real relationship with my Father and because I do I think before leaping. Wow, could have used that relationship earlier in my life!

Yes Mama truly was a very wise woman. I carry her wisdom with me every day. I hope you have a Mama, Grandma or someone special that shares her nuggets of wisdom with you. Most importantly, I hope you'll listen so that you can avoid the pitfalls of an unhealthy relationship.

About the Author

Joyous Janice G. Pettigrew began actively writing in 2009 with her first book, Journey to a Fresh Start, "Releasing the Junk…Revealing the Jewels in which she candidly shared her experiences of overcoming domestic violence, abuse and sexual assault to founding with her husband the nonprofit Fresh Start for Women.

In 2015 she followed up with 'Walk the Talk…Live a Joyous Life' in which she encouraged the reader to learn the lessons from their 'Ah Ha' moments to develop a roadmap for success.

This third offering 'Mama Said', is just another tool to educate, empower and inspire the reader. Janice loves writing and encouraging others. She is available for workshops, seminars and retreats. Follow her on Twitter, LinkedIn and Facebook or email her at janicepettigrew@gmail.com.

www.ingramcontent.com/pod-product-compliance
Lightning Source LLC
Chambersburg PA
CBHW071430040426
42445CB00012BA/1323